The Lincoln Memorial

Kristin L. Nelson

Lerner Publications Company
Minneapolis

To anyone who has fought for something he or she deeply believed in

Lerner Publications Company
A division of Lerner Publishing Group, Inc.
241 First Avenue North
Minneapolis, MN 55401 U.S.A.

Website address: www.lernerbooks.com

Library of Congress Cataloging-in-Publication Data

Nelson, Kristin L.
   The Lincoln Memorial / by Kristin L. Nelson.
        p.   cm. — (Lightning bolt books™ — Famous places)
   Includes index.
   ISBN 978-0-7613-6018-6 (lib. bdg. : alk. paper)
   1. Lincoln Memorial (Washington, D.C.)—Juvenile literature. 2. Lincoln, Abraham, 1809–1865—Monuments—Washington (D.C.)—Juvenile literature. 3. Washington (D.C.)—Buildings, structures, etc.—Juvenile literature. I. Title.
   F203.4.L73N45 2011
   975.3—dc22   2009039380

Manufactured in the United States of America
1 — BP — 7/15/10

Contents

Welcome to the Lincoln Memorial

Have you seen this building?
It's in Washington, D.C.

It's the Lincoln Memorial!
A memorial is something that
helps us remember a person
who died.

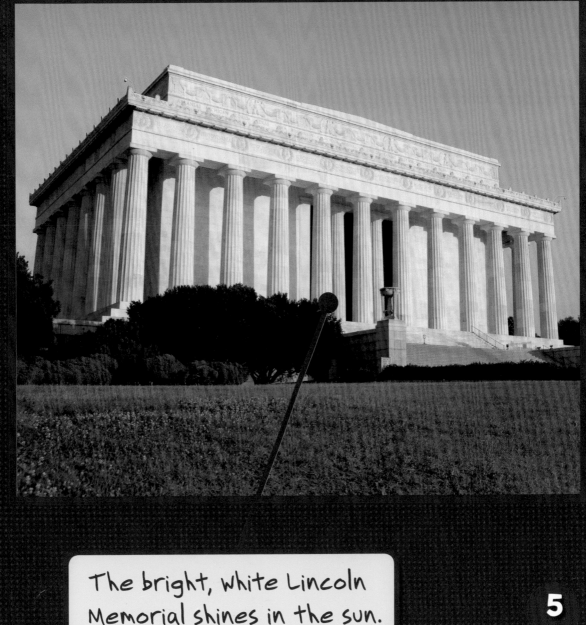

The bright, white Lincoln
Memorial shines in the sun.

The Lincoln Memorial was built to help people remember President Abraham Lincoln.

Lincoln's Life

Lincoln became a hero to many people. He led the country during the Civil War (1861–1865).

President Lincoln speaks to a crowd.

In the 1800s, most African Americans living in the southern United States were slaves. But African Americans lived freely in the north. Some people in the South feared Lincoln would end slavery in their states.

Slaves in South Carolina harvest sweet potatoes.

To keep the right to own slaves, southern states broke away. They formed a new country. The Civil War was fought between the northern states and the southern states.

Soldiers from northern states battle soldiers from southern states.

Lincoln reunited the country. He also made slavery illegal. Some people did not like his decisions. In 1865, a man shot Lincoln. He died the next day.

John Wilkes Booth shot Lincoln while he was watching a play.

Building the Memorial

People were sad after Lincoln died. They wanted to build a memorial. It would honor Lincoln's life.

Many people came out to see Lincoln's coffin.

In 1914, workers started building the memorial. They used a stone called marble.

Work begins on the Lincoln Memorial.

The workers put thirty-six columns around the building. Columns help support a building.

A crane lowers a part of a column into place.

The columns stand for the states. There were thirty-six states when Lincoln died.

The memorial is almost done!

Parts of Lincoln's speeches appear on the walls inside the memorial.

A grandmother and her grandson look at Lincoln's words.

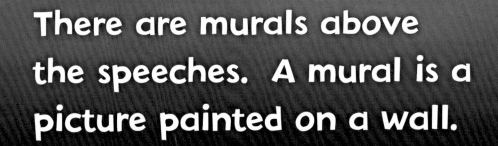

There are murals above the speeches. A mural is a picture painted on a wall.

A statue of Lincoln sits in the center of the memorial.

A sculptor named
Daniel Chester French
made the sculpture.

French carved the statue from twenty-eight pieces of marble. He put the pieces together like parts of a puzzle.

French stands among pieces of the Lincoln statue.

The statue was 19 feet (6 meters) tall when it was finished. That's taller than three men standing on one another's shoulders!

Lincoln's statue is huge compared to these visitors!

In 1922, the Lincoln Memorial was complete.

People listen to speeches on the day the Lincoln Memorial was opened to the public.

Visiting the Memorial

The **Lincoln Memorial** is a place for people to gather and talk about ideas.

In 1963, Martin Luther King Jr. gave a speech on the steps of the memorial.

Martin Luther King Jr. speaks to a crowd of two hundred thousand people at the Lincoln Memorial.

King told Americans about his dream that all people would one day have equal rights.

Martin Luther King Jr. waves to the crowd after his 1963 speech.

Millions of people visit the Lincoln Memorial every year.

Visitors enjoy looking into the Reflecting Pool outside.

The Reflecting Pool is lined with sidewalks and trees.

The Lincoln Memorial still reminds us of Lincoln's work to keep the country together. And it stands for his hope that its people will always be free.

Washington, D.C., Area

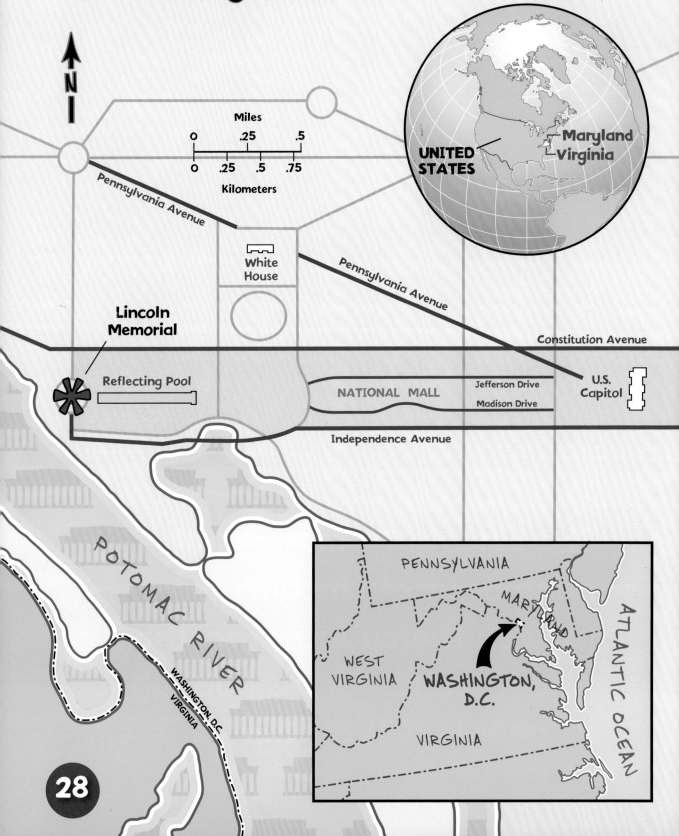

N

Miles
0   .25   .5

Kilometers
0   .25   .5   .75

Pennsylvania Avenue

White House

Pennsylvania Avenue

Lincoln Memorial

Constitution Avenue

Reflecting Pool

NATIONAL MALL

Jefferson Drive

Madison Drive

U.S. Capitol

Independence Avenue

POTOMAC RIVER

WASHINGTON, D.C.
VIRGINIA

UNITED STATES

Maryland
Virginia

PENNSYLVANIA

MARYLAND

WEST VIRGINIA

WASHINGTON, D.C.

VIRGINIA

ATLANTIC OCEAN

Fun Facts

- Workers started building the memorial on February 12, 1914. That day would have been Lincoln's 105th birthday!

- The Reflecting Pool in front of the memorial is more than 2,000 feet (610 m) long.

- Daniel Chester French used molds of Lincoln's hands and face to make the statue. A mold is a copy of the shape of something.

- The murals in the Lincoln Memorial are each 60 feet (18 m) long and 12 feet (4 m) tall.

- Lincoln's son Robert Todd Lincoln was the guest of honor at the memorial's opening in 1922.

Glossary

Civil War: the American war between the North and the South

column: a tall support for a building

marble: a hard stone with colored patterns

memorial: a place, event, or thing that helps remind us of a person who died

mural: a large picture painted on a wall

sculptor: an artist who carves objects out of wood or stone

slavery: one person or group's treatment of another person as property

statue: a copy carved in stone or wood of a person or thing

Further Reading

D'Aulaire, Ingri, and Edgar Parin D'Aulaire. *Abraham Lincoln.* San Luis Obispo, CA: Beautiful Feet Books, 2008.

Enchanted Learning: The Lincoln Memorial
http://www.enchantedlearning.com/history/us/monuments/lincolnmemorial

Hayden, Kate. *Amazing Buildings.* New York: DK Publishing, 2003.

King Jr., Martin Luther. *I Have a Dream.* New York: Scholastic, 2007.

National Park Service: Lincoln Memorial
http://www.nps.gov/linc/index.htm

Nelson, Kristin L. *The Washington Monument.* Minneapolis: Lerner Publications Company, 2011.

Index

Photo Acknowledgments

The images in this book are used with the permission of: © iStockphoto.com/Aimin Tang, p. 2; © iStockphoto.com/S. Greg Panosian, p. 4; © iStockphoto.com/Gary Blakeley, p. 5; National Archives, pp. 6 (111-B-3656), 13 (121-BS-103G-1), 19 (42-M-J-1); © George Eastman House/Hulton Archive/Getty Images, p. 7; © Louie Psihoyos/Science Faction/CORBIS, p. 8; Library of Congress, pp. 9 (LC-DIG-pga-01842), 11 (LC-DIG-ppmsca-19202), 12 (LC-DIG-hec-05419), 14 (LC-DIG-hec-07003), 21 (LC-DIG-hec-14448); © Bettmann/CORBIS, pp. 10, 18; © Stephen Voss/Alamy, p. 15; © Gregory F. Maxwell, Courtesy of Wikimedia Foundation, Inc., p. 16; © iStockphoto.com/Russell McBride, p. 17; © Ping Amranand/SuperStock, p. 20; © Stock Connection Blue/Alamy, p. 22; AP Photo/File, p. 23; © AFP/Getty Images, p. 24; © Wayne Grundy/Alamy, p. 25; © joeysworld.com/Alamy, p. 26; © age fotostock/SuperStock, pp. 27, 30; © Laura Westlund/Independent Picture Service, p. 28; © iStockphoto.com/Tom Marvin, p. 31.

Front cover: © Allan Baxter/Digital Vision/Getty Images.